KIRBY WI
FLOYD BROWN

Say the RIGHT Thing

Talk Radio's Favorite Conservative Quotes, Notes and Gloats

Merril Press
BELLEVUE, WASHINGTON

Say the RIGHT Thing

First Edition
Published by Merril Press

Typeset in Garamond by Merril Press. Cover design by
Northwoods Studio.

Additional copies of this book may be ordered from Merril Press
at $14.95 each. Merril Press is an independent publisher and
distributor of books to the trade, P.O. Box 1682, Bellevue, Washington 98009. Telephone 425-454-7009.

Citizens United is a non-profit, non-partisan educational organization based in Fairfax, Virginia. Citizens United can supply
additional copies of this book from 4101 Chain Bridge Road,
Suite 312, Fairfax, Virginia 22030. Telephone, 703-352-4788 or
1-800-362-4788. Website www.citizensunited.org.

LIBRARY OF CONGRESS CATALOGING-IN-PUBLICATION DATA
Wilbur, Kirby, 1953-
    Say the right thing : talk radio's favorite conservative quotes,
notes, and gloats / Kirby Wilbur, Floyd Brown
        p.   cm.
    ISBN 0-936783-22-2
    1. Conservatism--Quotations, maxims, etc. I. Brown. Floyd,
1961-. II. Title.
PN6084.C56W55   1998
320.52--dc21
                                            98-51772
                                              CIP

PRINTED IN THE UNITED STATES OF AMERICA

Dick—
Thank you for listening
Never give in!
Kirby

Say the RIGHT Thing

Dick—
Enjoy the wisdom
in those pages!
God Bless!
Floyd G. Brown

TABLE OF CONTENTS

EDITORS' INTRODUCTION

Collections of quotations have always been a favorite of ours. Together, we have over 50 years of political experience, a significant portion of which has been spent in debate, speeches and hosting radio talk shows. There is nothing so satisfying in those pursuits as finding the right quote to express more fully and adequately a thought, to convince the audience or to disarm an opponent.

Indeed, great quotes have a flavor you retain long after your initial contact, like the lingering taste of delicious chocolate, perfectly prepared steak or a fine cigar, tastes never experienced by the politically correct. They lie at the tip of your tongue, at the entrance to your mind, ready for instant recall when needed.

So, over the nearly 18 years of friendship we have traded many of our favorite quotes and quote books. This book is our attempt to share with you many of the nuggets of wisdom we have enjoyed over the years.

So, why another quote book? Simply because the standard collections have a severe bias against conservatives (check the index for Goldwater, Reagan or Thatcher in Bartlett's or Oxford sometime), and the few attempts in the past to compile a conservative collection have been feeble and woefully inadequate. We wanted to contribute to the movement—the cause—a volume with the best and widest selection of conservative thought and wisdom from the ages. One that an activist or bystander, novice or veteran could use, for research, speech writing, debate, entertainment or to clarify a thought. A book we hope will provide "the right thing to say," so to speak. You are now holding the results of our effort in your hands.

May you enjoy using it as much as we did compiling it. We hope it contributes in some way to your understanding of conservatism and your ability to communicate it.

We would like to extend a word of thanks to Erin Shannon, our research assistant, without whom this volume would not exist. We are indebted to Alan Gottlieb of Merril Press for seeing the merit in this collection and scheduling it for publication, and to Ron Arnold, editor in chief of Merril Press, for his guidance and support. We owe a special word of thanks to our wives, Trina Wilbur and Mary Beth Brown, and our families who understand and are always there. And finally we thank the great figures whose thoughts are in this book, who have spoken truths and insights that are universal and worth preserving.

May God bless you as He has blessed us, and may He continue to bless this great land with the gift of liberty. As Paul writes in the Second Chapter of Corinthians, Chapter 3, verse 17, "Where the spirit of the Lord is, there is liberty."

Kirby Wilbur
Floyd G. Brown
Seattle, Washington

AMERICA, AMERICANS, AND PATRIOTISM

The second day of July, 1776, will be the most memorable epoch in the history of America. I am apt to believe that it will be celebrated by succeeding generations as the great anniversary festival. It ought to be commemorated as the day of deliverance, by solemn acts of devotion to God Almighty. It ought to be solemnized with pomp and parade, with shows, games, sports, guns, bells, bonfires, and illustrations, from one end of the continent to the other, from this time forward forevermore.

—John Adams

...[T]he greatness of America is more than the sum total of its force of arms and the opulence of its economy: Its real power is its vision of an unlimited future.

—Barry Asmus

The making of an American begins at that point where he himself rejects all other ties, any other history, and himself adopts the vesture of his adopted land.

—James Baldwin

[The American flag] means the rising up of a valiant young people against an old tyranny to establish the most momentous doctrine that the world has ever known, or has since known—the right of men to their own selves and to their liberties.

—Henry Ward Beecher

America has believed that in differentiation, not in uniformity, lies the path of progress. It acted on this belief; it has advanced human happiness, and it has prospered.

—Louis D. Brandeis

We quarrel with no man for being a foreigner, but we recognize the moral right in no class of American citizens to train up their children to be foreigners, and then to claim for them all the rights, franchises, and immunities of American citizens.

—Orestes Augustus Brownson

The United States is like a gigantic boiler. Once the fire is lit under it, there is no limit to the power it can generate.

—Winston Churchill

The Americans took but little when they emigrated except what they stood up in and what they had in their souls. They came through, they tamed the wilderness, they became "a refuge for the oppressed from every land and clime."

—Winston Churchill

Patriotism is easy to understand in America. It means looking out for yourself by looking out for your country.

—Calvin Coolidge

Our country! In her intercourse with foreign nations may she always be right; but our country, right or wrong.

—Stephen Decatur

If all that Americans want is security they can go to prison. They'll have enough to eat, a bed and a roof over their heads. But if an American wants to preserve his dignity and his equality as a human being, he must not bow his neck to any dictatorial government.

—Dwight D. Eisenhower

America means opportunity, freedom, power.

—Ralph Waldo Emerson

America is another name for opportunity.

—Ralph Waldo Emerson

The superiority of the American system is eloquently proved by the pressure of people who want to crash our borders.

—William Feather

We Americans say that the Constitution made the nation. Well, the Constitution is a great document and we never would have been a nation without it, but it took more than that to make the nation. Rather it was our forefathers and foremothers, who made the Constitution and then made it work. The government they constructed did get great things out of them, but it was not the government primarily that put the great things into them. What put the great things into them was their home life, their religion, their sense of personal responsibility to Almighty God, their devotion to education, their love of liberty, their personal character.

—Harry Emerson Fosdick, D.D.

The greatness of the United States is due simply to this fact: Under the principle of individual liberty, human incentive has been given its widest scope.

—Crawford H. Greenewalt

Ours is a country deliberately founded on a good idea.

—John Gunther

In the great fulfillment we must have a citizenship less concerned about what the government can do for it and more anxious about what it can do for the nation.

—Warren G. Harding

The patriot, like the Christian, must learn that to bear revilings and persecutions is a part of his duty.

—Thomas Jefferson

The policy of the American government is to leave their citizens free, neither restraining nor aiding them in their pursuits.

—Thomas Jefferson

A man who hates America hates humanity.

—Paul Johnson

If a man is going to be an American at all let him be so without any qualifying adjectives; and if he is going to be something else let him drop the word American from his personal description.

—Henry Cabot Lodge

Americans never quit.

—General Douglas MacArthur

They are those, I know, who will say that the liberation of humanity, the freedom of man and mind, is nothing but a dream. They are right. It is the American dream.

—Archibald MacLeish

Americanism is not an accident of birth, but an achievement in terms of worth. Government does not create Americanism, but Americanism creates Government. Americanism is not a race, but a vision, a hope and an ideal.

—Louis I. Mann

Education is the indispensable means by which the ideas of the men who founded the American Republic can be disseminated and perpetuated. Only through education can the people be kept from becoming greedy and ignorant, from degenerating into a populace incapable of self-government. It is only by education, religion, and morality that the people can save themselves from becoming a willing instrument of their own debasement and ruin. The American Republic will endure only as long as the ideas of the men who founded it continue dominant.

—Daniel L. Marsh

We Americans are the peculiar, chosen people—the Israel of our time—we bear the ark of liberties of the world.

—Herman Melville

To be a good American means to understand the simple principles on which our nation was founded, to observe them in our daily life and to fight for them.

—Newbold Morris

[P]art of the inner architecture of the American ideal of freedom has been the profound conviction that only a virtuous people can be free.

—John Courtney Murray

The love of country is the first virtue in a civilized man.

—Napoleon I

The things that will destroy America are prosperity at any price, peace at any price, safety first instead of duty first, the love of soft living and the get-rich-quick feeling of living.

—Arthur Radford

Americans were the first to understand that wealth has to be created.

—Ayn Rand

I've always believed that this land was set aside in an uncommon way, that a divine plan placed this great continent between the oceans to be found by a people from every corner of the earth who had a special love of faith, freedom and peace.

—Ronald Reagan

Entrepreneurs share a faith in a bright future. They have a clear vision of where they are going and what they are doing, and they have a pressing need to succeed. If I didn't know better, I would be tempted to say that "entrepreneur" is another world for America.

—Ronald Reagan

America is too great for small dreams.

—Ronald Reagan

To divide along the lines of section or caste or creed is unAmerican.

—Theodore Roosevelt

There is no room in this country for hyphenated Americans.... The one absolutely certain way of bringing this nation to ruin, of preventing all possibility of it continuing to be a nation at all, would be to permit it to become a tangle of squabbling nationalities.

—Theodore Roosevelt

The man who loves other countries as much as his own stands on a level with the man who loves other women as much as he loves his own wife.

—Theodore Roosevelt

Americanism is a question of principle, of purpose, of Idealism or Character; it is not a matter of birthplace or creed or line of descent.

—Theodore Roosevelt

We have room for but one language here and that is the English language, and we intend to see that the crucible turns our people out as Americans, and not as dwellers of a polyglot boarding-house.

—Theodore Roosevelt

There can be no fifty-fifty Americanism in this country. There is room here only for 100 percent Americanism, only for those who are Americans and nothing else.

—Theodore Roosevelt

Our country...when right, to be kept right; when wrong, to be put right.

—Carl Schurz

America rests upon four cornerstones: the English Bible, the English language, the common law, and the tradition of liberty.

—Odell Shepard

Our forefathers gave us a system of government which has produced greater liberties and higher living standards than ever before experienced in the history of the world. As citizens it is our duty and our responsibility to do our utmost to protect that system and to provide moral leadership for the rest of the world.

—George E. Stringfellow

There is the National flag. He must be cold, indeed who can look upon its folds rippling in the breeze without pride of country.... If in a foreign land, the flag is companionship. White is for purity; red for valor; blue for justice.

—Charles Sumner

The great advantage of the American is that he has arrived at a state of democracy without having to endure a democratic revolution and that he is born free without having to become so.

—Alexis de Tocqueville

The United States is not a nation of people which in the long run allows itself to be pushed around.

—Dorothy Thompson

The United States is the only great and populous nation-state and world power whose people are not cemented by ties of blood, race or original language. It is the only world power which recognizes but one nationality of its citizens—American—while lacking the ties of blood, tribal kinship, original language, long-established culture, which contribute so much to national cohesion. How can such a union be maintained except through some idea which involves loyalty?

—Dorothy Thompson

My kind of loyalty was loyalty to one's country, not to its institutions or its officeholders.

—Mark Twain

The name of American, which belongs to you in your national capacity, must always exalt the just pride of patriotism more than any appellation derived from local discriminations. With slight shades of difference, you have the same religion, manners, habits and political principles. You have in common cause fought and triumphed together.

—George Washington

Let our object be, OUR COUNTRY, OUR WHOLE COUNTRY, AND NOTHING BUT OUR COUNTRY. And, by the blessing of God, may that country itself become a vast and splendid monument, not of oppression and terror, but of wisdom, of peace, and of liberty, upon which the world may gaze with admiration forever.

—Daniel Webster

I shall know but one country. The ends I aim at shall be my country's, my God's, and Truth's. I was born an American; I live an American; I shall die an American.

—Daniel Webster

A man who thinks of himself as belonging to a particular national group in America has not yet become an American and the man who goes among you to trade upon your nationality is no worthy son to live under the Stars and Stripes.

—Woodrow Wilson

Sometimes people call me an idealist. Well, that is the way I know I am an American. America is the only idealist nation in the world.

—Woodrow Wilson

BUREAUCRACY

The perfect bureaucrat everywhere is the man who manages to make no decisions and escape all responsibility.

—Brooks Atkinson

Too often I find that the volume of paper expands to fill the available briefcases.

—Jerry Brown

How prophetic L'Enfant was when he laid out Washington as a city that goes around in circles!

—John Mason Brown

There is no surer method of economizing and saving money than in the reduction of the number of officials.

—Winston Churchill

Bureaucracy is the death of any achievement.

—Albert Einstein

The quality of legislation passed to deal with a problem is inversely proportional to the volume of media clamour that brought it on.

—G. Ray Funkhouser

Government defines the physical aspects of man by means
of the Printed Form, so that for every man in the flesh there
is an exactly corresponding man on paper.

—Jean Giraudoux

The power which a multiple millionaire, who may be my
neighbor and perhaps my employer, has over me is very
much less than that which the smallest fonctionnaire pos-
sesses who wields that coercive power of the state, and on
whose discretion it depends whether and how I am to be
allowed to live or to work.

—Friedrich von Hayek

The only thing that saves us from the bureaucracy is ineffi-
ciency. An efficient bureaucracy is the greatest threat to
liberty.

—Eugene J. McCarthy

One thing about bureaucrats is that they never swallow
their young. Leave them alone and you'll find them increasing every year.

—Robert G. Menzies

Where self-interest is suppressed, it is replaced by a burden-
some system of bureaucratic control that dries up the
wellsprings of initiative and creativity.

—P. J. O'Rourke

Bureaucracy defends the status quo long past the time when the quo has lost its status.

—Laurence J. Peter

Bureaucrats write memoranda both because they appear to be busy when they are writing and because the memos, once written, immediately become proof they were busy.

—Charles Peters

If you're going to sin, sin against God, not the bureaucracy; God will forgive you but the bureaucracy won't.

—Hyman Rickover

We can lick gravity, but sometimes the paperwork is overwhelming.

—Wernher von Braun

CAPITALISM AND ECONOMICS

A study of economics usually reveals that the best time to buy anything is last year.

—Marty Allen

You don't make the poor richer by making the rich poorer.

—Winston Churchill

The vice of capitalism is that it stands for the unequal sharing of blessings; whereas the virtue of socialism is that is stands for the equal sharing of misery.

—Winston Churchill

I am astonished to see how people are afraid to defend the capitalist system. The politicians are afraid, the newspapers are afraid. As a matter of fact the capitalist system is capable of sustained and searching defense.

—Winston Churchill

Is it better to have equality at the price of poverty or well-being at the price of inequality?

—Winston Churchill

There is no right to strike against the public safety by anybody, anywhere, any time.

—Calvin Coolidge

Civilization and profits go hand in hand.

—Calvin Coolidge

Economists think the poor need them to tell them that they are poor.

—Peter Drucker

The experience of the past leaves little doubt that every economic system must sooner or later rely upon some form of the profit motive to stir individuals and groups to productivity. Substitutes like slavery, police supervision, or ideological enthusiasm prove too unproductive, too expensive, or too transient.

—Will Durant

Most economic fallacies derive...from the tendency to assume that there is a fixed pie, that one party can gain only at the expense of another.

—Milton Friedman

Real poverty is less a state of income than a state of mind.

—George Gilder

A successful economy depends on the proliferation of the rich, on creating a large class of risk-taking men who are willing to shun the easy channels of a comfortable life in order to create new enterprise, win huge profits, and invest them again.

—George Gilder

If ignorance paid dividends, most Americans could make a fortune out of what they don't know about economics.

—Luther Hodges

You know, the only trouble with capitalism is capitalists; they're too damn greedy.

—Herbert Hoover

Practical men, who believe themselves to be quite exempt from any intellectual influences, are usually the slaves of some defunct economist.... It is ideas, not vested interests, which are dangerous for good or evil.

—John Maynard Keynes

Creation comes before distribution—or there will be nothing to distribute.

—Ayn Rand

The reality is that zero defects in products plus zero pollution plus zero risk on the job is equivalent to maximum growth of government plus zero economic growth plus runaway inflation.

—Dixie Lee Ray

Millions of individuals making their own decisions in the market-place will always allocate resources better than any centralized government planning process.

—Ronald Reagan

But the truth is that outside of its legitimate function, government does nothing as well or as economically as the private sector of the economy.

—Ronald Reagan

Economic progress, in capitalist society, means turmoil.

—Joseph Schumpeter

There is inherent in the capitalist system a tendency toward self-destruction.

—Joseph Schumpeter

If all economists were laid end to end, they would not reach a conclusion.

—George Bernard Shaw

Unfortunately good economics is not always perceived to be good politics.

—William Simon

No one would remember the Good Samaritan if he only had good intentions. He had money as well.

—Margaret Thatcher

Never in the history of human credit has so much been owed.

—Margaret Thatcher

The more is given, the less the people will work for themselves and the less they work, the more their poverty will increase.

—Leo Tolstoy

October. This is one of the peculiarly dangerous months to speculate in stocks in. The others are July, January, September, April, November, May, March, June, December, August and February.

—Mark Twain

CHARACTER, COURAGE, AND HONOR

A character standard is far more important than even a gold standard. The success of all economic systems is still dependent upon both righteous leaders and righteous people. In the last analysis, our national future depends upon our national character—that is, whether it is spiritually or materially minded.

—Roger Babson

I mean to live my life an obedient man, but obedient to God, subservient to the wisdom of my ancestors; never to the authority of political truths arrived at yesterday at the voting booth.

—William F. Buckley, Jr.

Right is right, even if nobody does it. Wrong is wrong even if everybody is wrong about it.

—G. K. Chesterton

He is a sheep in sheep's clothing. (On British Prime Minister Clement Attlee)

—Winston Churchill

He who ascends to the mountaintops shall find the loftiest peaks most wrapped with clouds and snow.

—Winston Churchill

Difficulties mastered are opportunities won.

—Winston Churchill

Courage is rightly esteemed the first of human
qualities…because it is the quality which guarantees all
others.

—Winston Churchill

Our difficulties and our dangers will not be removed by
closing our eyes to them.

—Winston Churchill

Forward then. Forward! Let us go forward without fear
into the future and let us dread naught when duty calls.

—Winston Churchill

Our inheritance of well-founded, slowly conceived codes of
honor, morals and manners, the passionate convictions
which so many hundreds of millions share together of the
principles of freedom and justice, are far more precious to
us than anything which scientific discoveries could bestow.

—Winston Churchill

I am not concerning myself about what history will think,
but contenting myself with the approval of a fellow named
Cleveland whom I have generally found to be a pretty good
sort of fellow.

—Grover Cleveland

My message to you is: Be courageous! I have lived a long time. I have seen history repeat itself again and again. I have seen many depressions in business. Always America has come out stronger and more prosperous. Be as brave as your fathers before you. Have faith! Go forward.

—Thomas Edison's Last Public Message

Courage is contagious. When a brave man takes a stand, the spines of others are often stiffened.

—Billy Graham

One man with courage makes a majority.

—Andrew Jackson

In matters of principle, stand like a rock; in matters of taste, swim with the current.

—Thomas Jefferson

When a man assumes a public trust, he should consider himself as public property.

—Thomas Jefferson

Any dangerous spot is tenable if brave men will make it so.

—John F. Kennedy

If we as Americans show the same courage and common sense that motivated the men who sat at Philadelphia and gave us the Declaration of Independence and later the Constitution of the United States, there is no domestic problem we cannot solve and there is no foreign foe we need ever fear.

—William F. Knowland

In a sort of ghastly way we remove the organ and demand the function. We make men without chests and expect of them virtue and enterprise. We laugh at honour and are shocked to find traitors in our midst. We castrate and bid the geldings be fruitful.

—C. S. Lewis

Courage is not simply one of the virtues, but the form of every virtue at the testing point.

—C. S. Lewis

Nearly all men can stand adversity, but if you want to test a man's character, give him power.

—Abraham Lincoln

To sin by silence when they should protest makes cowards of men.

—Abraham Lincoln

Character is what you are in the dark.

—Dwight Lyman Moody

A man is not finished when he is defeated. He is finished when he quits.

—Richard M. Nixon

Never underestimate a man who overestimates himself.

—Franklin D. Roosevelt

No man is justified in doing evil on the grounds of expediency.

—Theodore Roosevelt

Far better it is to dare mighty things, to win glorious triumphs, even though checkered by failure, than to take rank with those poor spirits who neither enjoy much nor suffer much, because they live in the gray twilight that knows not victory nor defeat.

—Theodore Roosevelt

COMPASSION

We don't believe compassion should be measured by the size of the safety net, but by the number of rungs on the ladder of opportunity.

—Jack Kemp

We do not increase compassion by expanding it to cover anything. Instead, we kill a good word by making it mean too much, and nothing.

—Marvin Olasky

Welfare's purpose should be to eliminate, as far as possible, the need for its own existence.

—Ronald Reagan

CONSERVATIVES AND CONSERVATISM

Conservative: A statesman who is enamored of existing evils, as distinguished from the Liberal, who wishes to replace them with others.

—Ambrose Bierce

Conservatism is the politics of reality.

—William F. Buckley, Jr.

Conservatism is the tacit acknowledgment that all that is finally important in human experience is behind us; that the crucial explorations have been undertaken, and that it is given to man to know what are the great truths that emerged from them.

—William F. Buckley, Jr.

If the Conservative is less anxious than his Liberal brethren to increase Social Security "benefits," it is because he is more anxious than his Liberal brethren that people be free throughout their lives to spend their earnings when and as they see fit.

—Barry Goldwater

The conscience of the Conservative is pricked by anyone who would debase the dignity of the individual human being. Today, therefore, he is at odds with dictators who rule by terror, and equally with those gentler collectivists who ask our permission to play God with the human race.

—Barry Goldwater

What is conservatism? Is it not adherence to the old and tried, against the new and untried?

—Abraham Lincoln

Somehow liberals have been unable to acquire from life what conservatives seem to be endowed with at birth: namely, a healthy skepticism of the powers of government agencies to do good.

—Daniel P. Moynihan

Conservatism is primarily based on a proper recognition of human limitations.

—Lewis B. Namier

To be conservative, then, is to prefer the familiar to the unknown, to prefer the tried to the untried, fact to mystery, the actual to the possible, the limited to the unbounded, the near to the distant, the sufficient to the superabundant, the convenient to the perfect, present laughter to utopian bliss.

—Michael Oakeshott

Republicans believe every day is the Fourth of July, but Democrats believe every day is April 15.

—Ronald Reagan

A conservative is a liberal who was mugged the night before.

—Frank L. Rizzo

[Conservatism] is hardly more than an instinctive belief that today's society is built on several thousand years and that in those years men have found things they should fasten to.

—*Wall Street Journal* editorial, April 29, 1955

DEMOCRACY

The only legitimate right to govern is an express grant of power from the governed.

—William Henry Harrison

Every government degenerates when trusted to the rulers of the people alone. The people themselves therefore are its only safe depositories.

—Thomas Jefferson

...[Y]ou may believe fallen man to be so wicked that not one of them can be trusted with any irresponsible power over his fellows. That I believe to be the true ground of Democracy.

—C. S. Lewis

As I would not be a slave, so I would not be a master. This expresses my idea of democracy.

—Abraham Lincoln

"The consent of the governed" is more than a safeguard against ignorant tyrants: it is an insurance against benevolent despots as well.

—Walter Lippmann

Democracy is a device that insures we shall be governed no better than we deserve.

—George Bernard Shaw

Democracy substitutes selection by the incompetent many for appointment by the corrupt few.

—George Bernard Shaw

Democracy means simply the bludgeoning of the people by the people for the people.

—Oscar Wilde

EQUALITY

The only stable state is the one in which all men are equal before the law.

—Aristotle

The defect of equality is that we only desire it with our superiors.

—Henry Becque

We clamor for equality chiefly in matters in which we ourselves cannot hope to obtain excellence.

—Eric Hoffer

Your levelers wish to level down as far as themselves; but they cannot bear leveling up to themselves.

—Samuel Johnson

There can never be human happiness in a society that imposes a rule of "equality" which disregards merit and rewards incompetence.

—David Lawrence

For the reason that we are equal before God, we are made equal before the law of this land. And when you have said that, you have summed up and tied with a bowknot the complete American doctrine of equality.

—Clarence E. Manion

The passion for equality produces uniformity which produces mediocrity.

—Alexis de Tocqueville

FAITH AND GOD

He is a self-made man, and worships his creator.

—John Bright

The crisis of the Western world exists to the degree in which it is indifferent to God.

—Whittaker Chambers

The idea of liberty has ultimately a religious root; that is why men find it so easy to die for and so difficult to define.

—G. K. Chesterton

The danger of loss of faith in God is not that one will believe in nothing, but rather that one will believe in anything.

—G. K. Chesterton

The Christian ideal has not been tried and found wanting. It has been found difficult, and left untried.

—G. K. Chesterton

Moral collapse follows upon spiritual collapse.

—C. S. Lewis

Let us have faith that right makes might, and in that faith let us to the end do our duty as we understand it.

—Abraham Lincoln

Men must be governed by God or they will be ruled by tyrants.

—William Penn

When civilizations fail, it is almost always man who has failed—not in his body, not in his fundamental equipment and capacities, but in his will, spirit and mental habits.... Men—and civilization—live by their beliefs and die when their beliefs pass over into doubt.

—Philip Lee Ralph

The greatest asset of man, a business or a nation is faith.

The men who built this country and those who made it prosper during its darkest days were men whose faith in its future was unshakable.

Men of courage, they dared to go forward despite all hazards; men of vision, they always looked forward, never backward.

—Thomas J. Watson

FOREIGN POLICY AND DIPLOMACY

Diplomacy is the art of saying "Nice doggie!" till you can find a rock.

—Wynn Catlin

An appeaser is one who feeds a crocodile—hoping it will eat him last.

—Winston Churchill

Close alliance with despots are never safe for free states.

—Demosthenes

Foreign policy must be clear, consistent and confident.

—Dwight D. Eisenhower

The foreign policy adopted by our government is to do justice to all, and to submit to wrong by none.

—Andrew Jackson

You can always survive a mistake in domestic affairs but you can get killed by one made in foreign policy.

—John F. Kennedy

In order to be a diplomat one must speak a number of languages, including double-talk.

—Carey McWilliams

A foreign policy derived from the national interest is in fact morally superior to a foreign policy inspired by universal moral principles

—Hans Morgenthau

Diplomacy is letting someone else have your way.

—Lester B. Pearson

The ultimate determinant in the struggle now going on for the world will not be bombs and rockets but a test of wills and ideas—a trial of spiritual resolve; the values we hold, the beliefs we cherish and the ideas to which we are dedicated.

—Ronald Reagan

Foreign relations is an open book—generally a checkbook.

—Will Rogers

Diplomats are just as essential to starting a war as soldiers are for finishing it.... You take diplomacy out of war, and the thing would fall flat in a week.

—Will Rogers

The RIGHT Thing to Say

A diplomat is a person who can tell you to go to hell in such a way that you actually look forward to the trip.

—Caskie Stinnett

I think every nation has a right to establish that form of government, under which it conceives it may live most happy; provided it infracts no right, or is not dangerous to others; and that no governments ought to interfere with the internal concerns of another, except for the security of what is due to themselves.

—George Washington

FREEDOM AND LIBERTY

Liberty is not a means to a higher political end. It is itself the highest political end.

—Lord Acton

Liberty is the delicate fruit of a ripe civilization.

—Lord Acton

Liberty and good government do not exclude each other; and there are excellent reasons why they should go together.

—Lord Acton

Increase of freedom in the State may sometimes promote mediocrity, and give vitality to prejudice; it may even retard useful legislation, diminish the capacity for war, and restrict the boundaries of Empire.... A generous spirit prefers that his country should be poor, and weak, and of no account, but free, rather than powerful, prosperous and enslaved.

—Lord Acton

There is danger from all men. The only maxim of a free government ought to be to trust no man living with power to endanger the public liberty.

—John Adams

The moment the idea is admitted into society that property is not as sacred as the laws of God, and that there is not a force of law and public justice to protect it, anarchy and tyranny commence. If "Thou shalt not covet" and "Thou shalt not steal" were not commandments from Heaven, they must be made inviolable precepts in every society before it can be civilized or free.

—John Adams

Nip the shoots of arbitrary power in the bud, is the only maxim which can ever preserve the liberties of any people.

—John Adams

If ye love wealth greater than liberty, the tranquility of servitude greater than the animating contest for freedom, go home from us in peace. Crouch down and lick the hand that feeds you, and may posterity forget that ye were once our countrymen.

—Samuel Adams (to Tories)

Liberty is always unfinished business.

—American Council for Civil Liberties

To be truly free, it takes more determination, courage, introspection and restraint than to be in shackles.

—Pietro Belluschi

Freedom is when one hears the bell at seven o'clock in the morning and knows it is the milkman and not the Gestapo.

—Georges Bidault

Experience should teach us to be most on our guard to protect liberty when the government's purposes are beneficent.

—Louis D. Brandeis

Men born to freedom are naturally alert to repel invasion of their liberty by evil-minded rulers. The greatest dangers to liberty lurk in insidious encroachment by men of zeal, well-meaning but without understanding.

—Louis D. Brandeis

The true danger is when liberty is nibbled away, for expedience, and by parts.

—Edmund Burke

The effect of liberty on individuals is that they may do what they please: we ought to see what it will please them to do, before we risk congratulations.

—Edmund Burke

The people never give up their liberties but under some delusion.

—Edmund Burke

It is ordained in the eternal constitution of things that men of intemperate minds cannot be free. Their passions forge their fetters.

—Edmund Burke

It is better to cherish virtue and humanity, by leaving much to free will, even with some loss to the object, than to attempt to make men mere machines and instruments of a political benevolence. The world on the whole will gain by a liberty, without which virtue cannot exist.

—Edmund Burke

Men are qualified for civil liberty in exact proportion to their disposition to put moral chains upon their own appetites; in proportion as their love of justice is above their rapacity; in proportion as their soundness and sobriety of understanding is above their vanity and presumption; in proportion as they are more disposed to listen to the counsels of the wise and good, in preference to the flattery of knaves.

—Edmund Burke

Among a people generally corrupt liberty cannot long exist.

—Edmund Burke

It is harder to preserve than to obtain liberty.

—John C. Calhoun

Freedom is nothing else but a chance to be better.

—Albert Camus

The Republic may not give wealth or happiness; she has not promised these. It is the freedom to pursue these, not their realization, which the Declaration of Independence claims.

—Andrew Carnegie

Liberty is one of the choicest gifts that heaven hath bestowed upon man, and exceeds in volume all the treasures which the earth contains within its bosom or the sea covers. Liberty, as well as honor, man ought to preserve at the hazard of his life, for without it, life is insupportable.

—Miguel de Cervantes

The more man's choice is free, the more likely it is to be wise and fruitful not only to the chosen but to the community in which he dwells.

—Winston Churchill

All the greatest things are simple and can be expressed in a single world: Freedom, Justice, Honor, Duty, Mercy, Hope.

—Winston Churchill

We do not believe in having happiness imposed upon us.

—José Correa

The condition upon which God hath given liberty to man is eternal vigilance.

—John Philpot Curran

Freedom is the right to be wrong, not the right to do wrong.

—John G. Diefenbaker

When liberty becomes license, dictatorship is near.

—Will Durant

The history of free men is never really written by chance but by choice—their choice.

—Dwight D. Eisenhower

Freedom is a noble thing.
Who loseth his freedom, he loseth all.
Who hath freedom hath all sufficient.
Freedom and liberty should not be sold for all the gold and silver in the world.

—English proverbs, c.1375-1484

Only the educated are free.

—Epictetus

It is a fair summary of history to say that the safeguards of liberty have frequently been forged in cases involving not very nice people.

—Felix Frankfurter

The history of liberty has largely been the history of the observance of procedural safeguards.

—Felix Frankfurter

Those who would give up essential liberty to purchase a little temporary safety deserve neither liberty nor safety.

—Benjamin Franklin

Liberty will not descend to a people, people must raise themselves to liberty; it is a blessing that must be earned before it can be enjoyed.

—Benjamin Franklin

Where liberty dwells, there is my country.

—Benjamin Franklin

A society that puts equality...ahead of freedom will end up with neither equality nor freedom.

—Milton Friedman

History suggests that capitalism is a necessary condition for political freedom.

—Milton Friedman

If you believe in a free society, be worthy of a free society.

—John W. Gardner

Let your motto be resistance, resistance, RESISTANCE!
No oppressed people have ever secured their liberty without
resistance.

—Henry Highland Garnet

Extremism in the defense of liberty is no vice…. Moderation in the pursuit of justice is no virtue.

—Barry Goldwater

Those who seek to live your lives for you, to take your
liberty in return for relieving you of yours, those who
elevate the state and downgrade the citizen, must see ultimately a world in which earthly power can be substituted
for divine will. And this nation was founded upon the
rejection of that notion and upon the acceptance of God as
the author of freedom.

—Barry Goldwater

If dictatorship is the concentration of power, freedom
consists in its diffusion.

—Lord Hailsham

Liberty dies in the hearts of men and women: when it dies
there, no constitution, no law, no court can save it.

—Learned Hand

A society in which men recognize no check upon their
freedom soon becomes a society where freedom is the
possession of only a savage few.

—Learned Hand

See to the government. See that the government does not acquire too much power. Keep a check upon your rulers. Do this, and liberty is safe.

—William Henry Harrison

Liberty not only means that the individual has both the opportunity and the burden of choice; it also means that he must bear the consequences of his actions and will receive praise or blame for them. Liberty and responsibility are inseparable. A free society will not function or maintain itself unless its members regard it as right that each individual occupy the position that results from his action and accept it as due to his own action.

—Friedrich von Hayek

The love of liberty is the love of others; the love of power is the love of ourselves.

—William Hazlitt

Guard with jealous attention to the public liberty. Suspect everyone who approaches that jewel. Unfortunately, nothing will preserve it but down-right force.

—Patrick Henry

I know not what course others may take, but as for me, give me liberty, or give me death!

—Patrick Henry

Liberties...depend on the silence of the law.

—Thomas Hobbes

The basic test of freedom is perhaps less in what we are free to do than in what we are free not to do.

—Eric Hoffer

There can be no freedom without freedom to fail.

—Eric Hoffer

It is better for a man to go wrong in freedom than to go right in chains.

—Thomas H. Huxley

One should never put on one's best trousers to go out to fight for freedom.

—Henrik Ibsen

The God who gave us life, gave us liberty at the same time: the hand of force may destroy but cannot disjoin them.

—Thomas Jefferson

The freedom and happiness of man...are the sole objects of all legitimate government.

—Thomas Jefferson

The boisterous sea of liberty indeed is never without a wave.

—Thomas Jefferson

The tree of liberty must be refreshed from time to time with the blood of patriots and tyrants. It is its natural manure.

—Thomas Jefferson

The natural progress of things is for liberty to yield and government to gain ground.

—Thomas Jefferson

I would rather be exposed to the inconveniences attending too much liberty than those attending too small a degree of it.

—Thomas Jefferson

No student of history can have any doubt that, in the long run, the direction of mankind is towards greater freedom.

—Paul Johnson

The essence of a free society is not so much the right to appoint as the right to remove.

—Paul Johnson

Political liberty is good only insofar as it produces private liberty.

—Samuel Johnson

There are no limits to our future if we don't put limits on our people.

—Jack F. Kemp

Every man has by nature the right to possess property as his own.

—Pope Leo XIII

Proclaim liberty throughout all the land unto all the inhabitants thereof.

—Leviticus 25:10

The real reason for democracy is... [m]ankind is so fallen that no man can be trusted with unchecked power over his fellows. Aristotle said that some people were only fit to be slaves. I do not contradict him. But I reject slavery because I see no men fit to be masters.

—C. S. Lewis

The very idea of freedom presupposes some objective moral law which overarches rulers and ruled alike... But if there is no Law of Nature, the ethos of any society is the creation of its rulers, educators and conditioners; and every creator stands above and outside his own creation.

—C. S. Lewis

What constitutes the bulwark of our own liberty and independence? It is not our crowning battlements, our bristling sea coasts, the guns of our war steamers, or the strength of our gallant and disciplined army.... Our reliance is in the love of liberty which God has implanted in us.... Destroy this spirit, and you have planted the seeds of despotism at your own doors. Familiarize yourselves with the chains of bondage and you prepare your own limbs to wear them. Accustomed to trample on the rights of others, you have lost the genius of your own independence and become the fit subjects of the first cunning tyrant who rises among you.

—Abraham Lincoln

I believe that each individual is naturally entitled to do as he pleases with himself and the fruit of his labor, so far as it in no wise interferes with any other man's rights.

—Abraham Lincoln

The liberties we talk about defending today were established by men who took their conception of man from the great religious tradition of Western civilization, and the liberties we inherit can almost certainly not survive the abandonment of that tradition.

—Walter Lippmann

Private property was the original source of freedom. It still is its main bulwark.

—Walter Lippmann

No man is entitled to the blessings of freedom unless he be vigilant in its preservation.

—General Douglas MacArthur

The RIGHT Thing to Say

There is only one cure for the evils which newly acquired freedom produces and that cure is freedom.

—Thomas Macaulay

He is free who knows how to keep in his own hands the power to decide, at each step, the course of his life, and who lives in a society which does not block the exercise of that power.

—Salvador de Madariaga

As a man is said to have a right to his property, he may be equally said to have a property in his rights.

—James Madison

There are more instances of the abridgment of the freedom of the people, by gradual and silent encroachments of those in power, than by violent and sudden usurpations.

—James Madison

If a nation values anything more than freedom, it will lose its freedom; and the irony of it is that if it is comfort or money that it values more, it will lose that too.

—Somerset Maugham

Women's Liberation is just a lot of foolishness. It's the men who are discriminated against—they can't bear children. And no one's likely to do anything about that.

—Golda Meir

There is no freedom for the weak.

—George Meredith

Unless men are free to be vicious they cannot be virtuous.

—Frank Straus Meyer

The only purpose for which power can be rightfully exercised over any member of a civilized community, against his will, is to prevent harm to others. His own good, either physical or moral, is not a sufficient warrant.

—John Stuart Mill

A man who has nothing which he is willing to fight for, nothing which he cares more about than he does about his personal safety, is a miserable creature who has no chance of being free, unless made and kept so by the exertions of better men than himself.

—John Stuart Mill

The only freedom deserving the name, is that of pursuing our own good in our own way, so long as we do not attempt to deprive other of theirs, or impede their efforts to obtain it.

—John Stuart Mill

The liberty of the individual must be thus far limited; he must not make himself a nuisance to other people.

—John Stuart Mill

The love of power and the love of liberty are in eternal antagonism.

—John Stuart Mill

It is clear truth that those who barter away other men's liberty will soon care little for their own.

—James Otis

Those who expect to reap the blessing of freedom must, like men, undergo the fatigue of supporting it.

—Thomas Paine

Tyranny, like hell, is not easily conquered; yet we have this consolation with us, that the harder the conflict, the more glorious the triumph. What we obtain too cheap, we esteem too lightly.

—Thomas Paine

Man was not born to go down on his belly before the state.

—Alan Paton

Happiness is freedom, and freedom is courage.

—Pericles

Remember that prosperity can be only for the free, and that freedom is the sure possession of those alone who have the courage to defend it.

—Pericles

Eternal vigilance is the price for liberty.

—Wendell Phillips

Necessity is the plea for every infringement of human freedom. It is the argument of tyrants; it is the creed of slaves.

—William Pitt

There is no doubt that the real destroyer of the liberties of any people is he who spreads among them bounties, donations and largess.

—Plutarch

Freedom is the recognition that no single person, no single authority or government has a monopoly on truth, but that every individual life is infinitely precious, that every one of us put on this world has been put there for a reason and has something to offer.

—Ronald Reagan

I hope we have once again reminded people that man is not free unless government is limited. There's a clear cause and effect here that is as neat and predictable as a law of physics: as government expands, liberty contracts.

—Ronald Reagan

Freedom is as little lost in a day as won in a day.

—Jean Paul Richter

Freedom can not be bought for nothing; if you hold her precious, you must hold all else of little value.

—Lucius Annaeus Seneca

Liberty means responsibility. That is why most men dread it.

—George Bernard Shaw

Liberty is the possibility of doubting, the possibility of making a mistake, the possibility of searching and experimenting, the possibility of saying "NO" to any authority— literary, artistic, philosophic, religious, social, and even political.

—Ignazio Silone

The freedom of America is the freedom to live your own life and take your own chances.

—Thomas Sowell

If I want to be free from any other man's dictation, I must understand that I can have no other man under my control.

—W. G. Sumner

Ladies and gentlemen, I stand before you tonight in my green chiffon evening gown, my face softly made up, my fair hair softly waved.... The Iron Lady of the Western World? Me? A cold warrior? Well, yes—if that is how they wish to interpret my defence of the values and freedom fundamental to our way of life.

—Margaret Thatcher

Freedom under the law must never be taken for granted.

—Margaret Thatcher

When liberty is taken away by force it can be restored by force. When it is relinquished voluntarily by default it can never be recovered.

—Dorothy Thompson

The secret of Happiness is Freedom, and the secret of Freedom, Courage.

—Thucydides

Liberty, when it begins to take root, is a plant of rapid growth.

—George Washington

The contest for ages has been to rescue liberty from the grasp of executive power.

—Daniel Webster

God grants liberty only to those who love it, and are always ready to guard and defend it.

—Daniel Webster

Wherever public spirit prevails, liberty is secure.

—Noah Webster

The adherents of the various forms of socialism never tire in their efforts to make the State supreme. With the same zeal and with the weight of history on our side, we should become champions of personal freedom and the private way.

—Ernest T. Weir

Liberty is the only thing you cannot have unless you are willing to give it to others.

—William Allen White

Liberty has never come from the government. Liberty has always come from the subjects of it. The history of liberty is a history of resistance. The history of liberty is a history of limitations of governmental power, not the increase of it.

—Woodrow Wilson

If America is not to have free enterprise, then she can have no freedom of any sort whatever.

—Woodrow Wilson

If liberty has any meaning it means freedom to improve.

—Philip Wylie

THE FUTURE

It would be an unsound fancy and self-contradictory to expect that things which have never yet been done can be done except by means which have never yet been tried.

—Sir Francis Bacon

Never flinch, never weary, never despair.

—Winston Churchill

There is one cardinal rule: "Never Despair." That word is forbidden.

—Winston Churchill

What's past is prologue, what to come
In yours and my discharge.

—William Shakespeare

GENERAL MAXIMS

Today's mighty oak is just yesterday's little nut that held its ground.

—Anonymous

I do not suggest that you should not have an open mind, particularly as you approach college. But, don't keep your mind so open that your brains fall out.

—William J. Bennett

The concessions of the weak are the concessions of fear.

—Edmund Burke

When bad men combine, the good must associate; else they will fall one by one, an unpitied sacrifice in a contemptible struggle.

—Edmund Burke

There is, however, a limit at which forbearance ceases to be a virtue.

—Edmund Burke

When ancient opinions and rules of life are taken away, the loss cannot possibly be estimated. From that moment we have no compass to govern us, nor can we know distinctly to what port to steer.

—Edmund Burke

Our future is in our hands. Our lives are what we choose to make them.

—Winston Churchill

It is no use saying "We are doing our best." You have to succeed in doing what is necessary.

—Winston Churchill

The short road to ruin is to emulate...the methods of your adversary.

—Winston Churchill

Books in all their variety are often the means by which civilization may be carried triumphantly forward.

—Winston Churchill

The counsels of prudence and restraint may become the prime agents of mortal danger.

—Winston Churchill

It is better to be making the news than taking it, to be an actor rather than a critic.

—Winston Churchill

It is a fine thing to be honest, but it is also very important to be right.

—Winston Churchill

What most people call bad judgment is judgment which is different from theirs.

—Winston Churchill

He who wants to persuade should put his trust, not in the right argument but in the right word. The power of sound has always been greater than the power of sense.

—Joseph Conrad

Originality and a feeling of one's own dignity are achieved only through work and struggle.

—Feodor Dostoyevsky

A nation that values its privileges above its principles soon loses both.

—Dwight D. Eisenhower

We must all hang together, or assuredly we shall all hang separately.

—Benjamin Franklin

The middle of the road is where the white line is—and that's the worst place to drive.

—Robert Frost

An invasion of armies can be resisted, but not an idea whose time has come.

—Victor Hugo

The road to Hell is paved with good intentions.

—Karl Marx

An expert is somebody who is more than 50 miles away from home, has no responsibility for implementing the advice he gives, and shows slides.

—Edwin Meese III

The fear of life is the favorite disease of the twentieth century.

—William Lyon Phelps

To wear your heart on your sleeve isn't a very good plan; you should wear it inside, where it functions best.

—Margaret Thatcher

What is a cynic? A man who knows the price of everything, and the value of nothing.

—Oscar Wilde

Experience is the name everyone gives to their mistakes.

—Oscar Wilde

Life does not consist in thinking, it consists in acting.

—Woodrow Wilson

GOVERNMENT

As the happiness of the people is the sole end of government, so the consent of the people is the only foundation of it.

—John Adams

It gets harder and harder to support the government in the manner to which it has become accustomed.

—Anonymous

Government is the great fiction, through which everybody endeavors to live at the expense of everybody else.

—M. Frederic Bastiat

It is with government as with medicine. Its only business is the choice of evils. Every law is an evil, for every law is an infraction of liberty.

—Jeremy Bentham

The marvel of all history is the patience with which men and women submit to burdens unnecessarily laid upon them by their governments.

—William Borah

In a constitutional democracy the moral content of law must be given by the morality of the framer or legislator, never by the morality of the judge.

—Robert H. Bork

Washington is a pool of money surrounded by people who want some.

—David Brinkley

If everyone in the government would refuse to sign everything they couldn't read, everything would grind to a screeching halt.

—Jerry Brown

The great problem in government is that it never goes bankrupt.

—Jerry Brown

All modern revolutions have ended in a reinforcement of the power of the State.

—Albert Camus

Government is emphatically a machine: to the discontented a "taxing machine," to the contented a "machine for securing property."

—Thomas Carlyle

The office of government is not to confer happiness, but to give men opportunity to work out happiness for themselves.

—William Ellery Channing

The lessons of paternalism ought to be unlearned and the better lesson taught that while the people should patriotically and cheerfully support their Government its functions do not include the support of the people.

—Grover Cleveland

The admitted right of a government to prevent the influx of elements hostile to its internal peace and security may not be questioned, even where there is no treaty stipulation on the subject.

—Grover Cleveland

An oppressive government is more to be feared than a tiger.

—Confucius

The foundation of every state is the education of its youth.

—Diogenes

Everyone is always in favour of general economy and particular expenditure.

—Anthony Eden

There is far more danger in public than in private monopoly, for when Government goes into business it can always shift its losses to the taxpayers. Government never makes ends meet—and that is the first requisite of business.

—Thomas Edison

The less government we have, the better—the fewer laws, and the less confided power.

—Ralph Waldo Emerson

Governments never learn. Only people learn.

—Milton Friedman

The state, it cannot too often be repeated, does nothing, and can give nothing, which it does not take from somebody.

—Henry George

Government can have no more than two legitimate purposes—the suppression of injustice within the community, and the common defense against external invasion.

—William Godwin

A government that is big enough to give you all you want is big enough to take it all away.

—Barry Goldwater

The legitimate functions of government are actually conducive to freedom. Maintaining internal order, keeping foreign foes at bay, administering justice, removing obstacles to the free interchange of goods—the exercise of these powers makes it possible for men to follow their chosen pursuits with maximum freedom.

—Barry Goldwater

I fear Washington and centralized government more than I do Moscow.

—Barry Goldwater

It is no part of the State's duty to facilitate the spiritual redemption of rich men by impoverishing them in this life.

—John Grigg

Why has government been instituted at all? Because the passions of men will not conform to the dictates of reason and justice without constraint.

—Alexander Hamilton

The greatest danger to liberty today comes from the men who are most needed and most powerful in modern government, namely, the efficient expert administrators exclusively concerned with what they regard as public good.

—Friedrich von Hayek

No free government, or the blessings of liberty can be preserved to any people but by a firm adherence to justice, moderation, temperance, frugality, and virtue, and by a frequent recurrence to fundamental principles.

—Patrick Henry

If we fixed a hangnail the way our government fixes the economy, we'd slam a car door on it.

—Cullen Hightower

No matter how noble the objectives of a government, if it blurs decency and kindness, cheapens human life, and breeds ill will and suspicion it is an evil government.

—Eric Hoffer

What has always made the state a hell on earth has been precisely that man has tried to make it his heaven.

—Friedrich Holderlin

The general rule, at least, is that while property may be regulated to a certain extent, if regulation goes too far it will be recognized as taking.

—Oliver Wendell Holmes, Jr.

When the State endeavours to function as a charitable institution it does more harm than good.

—Arthur Hopkinson

The selfish wish to govern is often mistaken for a holy zeal in the cause of humanity.

—Elbert Hubbard

The purification of politics is an iridescent dream. Government is force.

—John James Ingalls

A wise and frugal government, which shall restrain men from injuring one another, shall leave them otherwise free to regulate their own pursuits of industry and improvement, and shall not take from the mouth of labor the bread it has earned. This is the sum of good government....

—Thomas Jefferson

My idea is that we should be made one nation in every case concerning foreign affairs, and separate ones in whatever is merely domestic.

—Thomas Jefferson

If the present Congress errs in too much talking, how can it be otherwise in a body to which people send 150 lawyers?

—Thomas Jefferson

I am not a friend to a very energetic government. It is always oppressive.

—Thomas Jefferson

I place economy among the first most important virtues, and public debt as the greatest dangers to be feared.... To preserve our independence, we must not let our rulers load us with perpetual profusion and servitude.... If we run into such debts, we must be taxed in our meat and drink, in our necessities and our comforts, in our labors and in our amusements.... If we can prevent the Government from wasting the labors of the people, under the pretense of caring for them, they will be happy.

—Thomas Jefferson

The legitimate powers of government extend to such acts only as are injurious to others.

—Thomas Jefferson

Were we directed from Washington when to sow, and when to reap, we should soon want bread.

—Thomas Jefferson

No, my friend, the way to have good and safe government, is not to trust it all to one, but to divide it among the many.

—Thomas Jefferson

I think we have more machinery of government than is necessary, too many parasites living on the labor of the industrious.

—Thomas Jefferson

My reading of history convinces me that most bad government results from too much government.

—Thomas Jefferson

The principle of our Government is that of equal laws and freedom of industry.

—Andrew Johnson

It is one of the dismal lessons of the twentieth century that, once a state is allowed to expand, it is almost impossible to contract it.

—Paul Johnson

The state had proved itself an insatiable spender, an unrivaled waster. It had also proved itself the greatest killer of all time. By the 1990's, state action had been responsible for the violent or unnatural deaths of some 125 million people during the century, more perhaps than it had succeeded in destroying during the whole of human history up to 1900. Its inhuman malevolence had more than kept pace with its growing size and expanding means.

—Paul Johnson

...[T]he urge to distribute wealth equally, and still more the belief that it can be brought about by political action, is the most dangerous of all popular emotions. It is the legitimization of envy of all the deadly sins the one which a stable society based on consensus should fear the most. The monster state is a source of many evils; but it is, above all, an engine of envy.

—Paul Johnson

Too often our Washington reflex is to discover a problem and then throw money at it, hoping it will somehow go away.

—Kenneth B. Keating

One of the things we have to be thankful for is that we don't get as much government as we pay for.

—Charles F. Kettering

A government is not legitimate merely because it exists.

—Jeane Kirkpatrick

The fact is that government cannot produce equality, and any serious effort to do so can destroy liberty and other social goods.

—Jeane Kirkpatrick

Because regulation uses the coercive power of government to alter outcomes, it diminishes individual liberty: people are persuaded by the threat of sanctions to act differently than they would otherwise.

—Jeane Kirkpatrick

The supply of government exceeds the demand.

—Lewis H. Lapham

The State exists simply to promote and to protect the ordinary happiness of human beings in this life. A husband and wife chatting over a fire, a couple of friends having a game of darts in a pub, a man reading a book in his own room or digging in his own garden—that is what the State is there for. And unless they are helping to increase and prolong and protect such moments, all the laws, parliaments, armies, courts, police, economics, *etc.*, are simply a waste of time.

—C. S. Lewis

The legitimate object of government, is to do for a community of people, whatever they need to have done, but can not do, at all, or can not, so well do, for themselves—in their separate, and individual capacities. In all that the people can individually do as well for themselves, government ought not to interfere.

—Abraham Lincoln

But what is government itself but the greatest of all reflections on human nature? If men were angels, no government would be necessary. If angels were to govern men, neither external controls nor internal controls on government would be necessary.

—James Madison

The powers delegated by the proposed Constitution to the federal government are few and defined. Those which are to remain in the State governments are numerous and indefinite.

—James Madison

No theoretical checks—no form of government, can render us secure. To suppose that any form of government will secure liberty or happiness without any virtue in the people is a chimerical idea.

—James Madison

In framing a government which is to be administered by men over men, the great difficulty lies in this: you must first enable government to control the governed; and in the next place oblige it to control itself.

—James Madison

Every nation has the government it deserves.

—Joseph de Maistre

Congress is so strange. A man gets up to speak and says nothing. Nobody listens—and then everybody disagrees.

—Boris Marshalov

The whole duty of government is to prevent crime and to preserve contracts.

—2nd Viscount Melbourne

Government is the only institution that can take a valuable commodity like paper, and make it worthless by applying ink.

—Ludwig von Mises

In large states public education will always be mediocre, for the same reason that in large kitchens the cooking is usually bad.

—Friedrich Nietzsche

Religion, morality, and knowledge being necessary to good government, and the happiness of mankind, schools and the means of education shall forever be encouraged.

—Northwest Ordinance

Giving money and power to government is like giving whiskey and car keys to teenage boys.

—P .J. O'Rourke

A little government and a little luck are necessary in life, but only a fool trusts either of them.

—P. J. O'Rourke

When government…becomes the principal source of aid and assistance in our society, [it is] proof that we're jerks, since we've decided that politicians are wiser, kinder and more honest than we are and that they, not we, should control the dispensation of eleemosynary goods and services.

—P. J. O'Rourke

The end of the government being the good of mankind points out its great duties: it is above all things to provide for the security, the quiet, the happy enjoyment of life, liberty, and property.

—James Otis

Government, even in its best state, is but a necessary evil; in its worst state, an intolerable one.

—Thomas Paine

Nationalization would seem to operate on the theory that a socialistic government can legislate unsuccessful people into prosperity by legislating successful people out of it.

—Cecil Palmer

The punishment suffered by the wise who refuse to take part in the government, is to live under the government of bad men.

—Plato

The end of the institution, maintenance and administration of government is to secure the existence of the body politic, to protect it, and to furnish the individuals who compose it with the power of enjoying in safety and tranquillity their natural rights and the blessings of life.

—Jacob Prout

Why are congressmen called public servants? You never see servants that anxious to keep their jobs.

—Robert Quillen

Anything that the private sector can do, the government can do it worse.

—Dixie Lee Ray

Government always finds a need for whatever money it gets.

—Ronald Reagan

It's time to reject the notion that advocating government programs is a form of personal charity. Generosity is a reflection of what one does with his or her own resources and not what he or she advocates the government to do with everyone's money.

—Ronald Reagan

There is no art which one government sooner learns of another than that of draining money from the pockets of the people.

—Ronald Reagan

Government does not solve problems; it subsidizes them.

—Ronald Reagan

The nine most terrifying words in the English language are, "I'm from the government and I'm here to help."

—Ronald Reagan

One of the greatest delusions in the world is the hope that the evils in this world are to be cured by legislation.

—Thomas B. Reed

A government which robs Peter to pay Paul can always depend on the support of Paul.

—George Bernard Shaw

Commerce and manufacturers, in short, can seldom flourish in any state in which there is not a certain degree of confidence in the justice of government.

—Adam Smith

The difference between Wall Street and Washington can be summed up simply and vividly. If the stock market crashed, the whole country would be impoverished. But if the federal government suddenly went poof, most Americans would be immediately enriched. The only losers would be the overclass.

—Joseph Sobran

The true aim of government is liberty.

—Baruch Spinoza

It is not the function of the State to make men happy. They must make themselves happy in their own way, and at their own risk.

—William Graham Sumner

For in reason, all government without the consent of the governed is the very definition of slavery.

—Jonathan Swift

The role of government is to strengthen our freedom—not deny it.

—Margaret Thatcher

Generals should never do anything that needs to be explained to a Senate committee—there is nothing one can explain to a Senate committee.

—Harry S. Truman

All communities are apt to look to government too much.... The framers of our excellent Constitution...wisely judged that the less government interferes with private pursuits the better for the general prosperity.

—Martin Van Buren

In general, the art of government consists in taking as much money as possible from one party of citizens to give to the other.

—Voltaire

Government is not reason, it is not eloquence—it is force! Like fire it is a dangerous servant and a fearful master; never for a moment should it be left to irresponsible action.

—George Washington

It is only the novice in political economy who thinks it is the duty of government to make its citizens happy. Government has no such office. To protect the weak and the minority from the impositions of the strong and the majority—to prevent any one from positively working to render the people unhappy...to do the labor not of an officious intermeddler in the affairs of men, but of a prudent watchman who prevents outrage—these are rather the proper duties of government.

—Walt Whitman

HISTORY

History is the sum total of things that could have been avoided.

—Konrad Adenauer

History does not repeat itself. Historians repeat each other.

—Arthur J. Balfour

People will not look forward to posterity, who never look backward to their ancestors.

—Edmund Burke

What is past cannot be rewritten, but it is within our power to rewrite the future.

—Catherine II

Study history, study history—in history lie all the secrets of statecraft.

—Winston Churchill

A good knowledge of history is a quiver full of arrows in debates.

—Winston Churchill

Everyone can recognize history when it happens. Everyone can recognize history after it has happened: but it is only the wise man who knows at the moment what is vital and permanent what is lasting and memorable.

—Winston Churchill

If the present tries to sit in judgment of the past, it will lose the future.

—Winston Churchill

Is it the only lesson of history that mankind is unteachable?

—Winston Churchill

Those who do not know history are forever condemned to repeat it.

—Will Durant

History is a voice forever sounding across the centuries the laws of right and wrong.

—James Anthony Froude

What experience and history teaches is this—that people and governments have never learnt anything from history or acted on principles deduced from it.

—Georg Friedrich Hegel

A generation which ignores history has no past—and no future.

—Robert A. Heinlein

I have but one lamp by which my feet are guided, and this is the lamp of experience. I know of no way of judging the future but by the past.

—Patrick Henry

A page of history is worth a volume of logic.

—Oliver Wendell Holmes

The more I study history, the more convinced I am that what happens is influenced as much by the willpower of key individuals as by the underlying pressure of collective forces.

—Paul Johnson

There are no inevitabilities in history.

—Paul Johnson

It is from numberless diverse acts of courage and belief that human history is shaped.

—Robert F. Kennedy

Few will have the greatness to bend history itself. But each of us can work to change a small portion of events, and in the total of all those acts will be written the history of this generation.

—Robert F. Kennedy

I predict that the twentieth century will spend a good deal of its time picking out of the wastebasket things that the nineteenth century threw into it.

—Ernest Renan

We are the heirs of the ages.

—Theodore Roosevelt

HUMAN NATURE

Knowledge of human nature is the beginning and end of political education.

—Henry Adams

Man is not the creature of circumstances. Circumstances are the creatures of men.

—Benjamin Disraeli

It is tempting to believe that social evils arise from the activities of evil men and that if only good men (like ourselves, naturally) wielded power, all would be well. That view requires only emotion and self-praise.

—Milton Friedman

It is natural to man to indulge in the illusions of hope. We are apt to shut our eyes against a painful truth and listen to the song of that siren, till she transforms us into beasts.

—Patrick Henry

IMMIGRATION

My whole family has been having trouble with immigrants ever since we came to this country.

—Edgar Y. Harburg

Immigration is the sincerest form of flattery.

—A.F.K. Organski

Every immigrant who comes here should be required within five years to learn English or leave the country.

—Theodore Roosevelt

INDIVIDUALISM

Where individual and corporate rights conflict, the political balance should usually be weighted in favour of the individual; for civilizations are created, and maintained, not by corporations, however benign, but by multitudes of individuals operating independently.

—Paul Johnson

Success does not so much depend on external help as on self-reliance.

—John Locke

It is always the individual who thinks. Society does not think any more than it eats or drinks.

—Ludwig von Mises

Besides the earth, man's principal resource is man himself.

—Pope John Paul II

JUDGES AND JUDICIARY

As a member of this court I am not justified in writing my private notions of policy into the Constitution, no matter how deeply I may cherish them or how mischievous I may deem their disregard.

—Felix Frankfurter

It is a very dangerous doctrine to consider the judges as the ultimate arbiters of all constitutional questions. It is one which would place us under the despotism of an oligarchy.

—Thomas Jefferson

The people can change Congress but only God can change the Supreme Court.

—George W. Norris

The decision of the courts on economic and social questions depend on their economic and social philosophy.

—Theodore Roosevelt

The thing to fear is not the law but the judge.

—Russian Saying

The judge is condemned when the guilty is acquitted.

—Publilius Syrus

LAW AND THE CONSTITUTION

Men are not hanged for stealing horses, but that horses may not be stolen.

—1st Marquess of Halifax

For a deadly blow let him pay with a deadly blow: it is for him who has done a deed to suffer.

—Aeschylus

The less people know about how sausages and laws are made, the better they'll sleep at night.

—Otto von Bismarck

Our Constitution was not written in the sands to be washed away by each wave of new judges blown in by each successive political wind.

—Hugo L. Black

Let the punishment match the offense.

—Marcus Cicero

The more laws, the less justice.

—Marcus Cicero

Moral principle is the foundation of law.

—Ronald D. Dworkin

He that smiteth a man, so that he die, shall be surely put to death.

—Exodus 21:12

The ordaining of laws in favor of one part of the nation, to the prejudice and oppression of another, is certainly the most erroneous and mistaken policy.

—Benjamin Franklin

If a man destroy the eye of another man, they shall destroy his eye.

—Hammurabi Code, ca. 2250 BC

The Constitution not only is, but ought to be what the judges say it is.

—Charles Evans Hughes

The execution of laws is more important than the making of them.

—Thomas Jefferson

In questions of power...let no more be heard of confidence in men, but bind him down from mischief by the chains of the Constitution.

—Thomas Jefferson

The Constitution of the United States is the result of the collected wisdom of our country.

—Thomas Jefferson

Law alone cannot make men see right.

—John F. Kennedy

A good constitution is infinitely better than the best despot.

—Thomas Macaulay

Every word [of the Constitution] decides a question between power and liberty.

—James Madison

Crime is rampant because the law-abiding, each of us, condone it, excuse it, permit it, submit to it. We permit and encourage it because we do not fight back, immediately, then and there, where it happens.

—Jeffrey Snyder

When the state is corrupt then the laws are most multiplied.

—Tacitus

LEADERSHIP

Lincoln was not great because he was born in a log cabin, but because he got out of it.

—James Truslow Adams

Nothing doeth more hurt in a state than that cunning men pass for wise.

—Francis Bacon

It is hard to look up to a leader who keeps his ear to the ground.

—James H. Boren

There is no limit to what the good man can do if he doesn't care who gets the credit.

—Judson B. Branch

The hinge of fate has made this nation leader in the struggle for the oppressed wherever darkness has fallen and the light of liberty has gone out.... So live, therefore, and so perform your part that free men across the future years will look back and say, "Here was a generation that did not seek security, but looked for opportunity."

—W. Norwood Brigance

Great men are the guide-posts and landmarks in the state.

—Edmund Burke

A disposition to preserve, and an ability to improve, taken together, would be my standard of a statesman.

—Edmund Burke

No great man lives in vain. The history of the world is but the biography of great men.

—Thomas Carlyle

Not armies, not nations, have advanced the race; but here and there, in the course of the ages, an individual has stood up and cast his shadow over the world.

—Edwin H. Chapin

Let us set up a standard which the brave and loyal can rally.

—Winston Churchill

The price of greatness is responsibility.

—Winston Churchill

If the bugle gives an indistinct sound, who will get ready for battle?

—1 Corinthians 14:8

You cannot choose your battlefield,/ The gods do that for you,/ But you can plant a standard/ Where a standard never flew.

—Nathalia Crane

A man who wants to lead the orchestra must turn his back on the crowd.

—James Crook

This Republic was not established by cowards; and cowards will not preserve it.

—Elmer Davis

The men who build the future are those who know that greater things are yet to come, and that they themselves will help bring them about. Their minds are illuminated by the blazing sun of hope. They never stop to doubt. They haven't time.

—Melvin J. Evans

The secret of all victory lies in the organization of the nonobvious. To accomplish great things, we must not only act, but also dream, not only plan, but also believe.

—Anatole France

Great hopes make great men.

—Thomas Fuller

The men who succeed best in public life are those who take the risk of standing by their own convictions.

—James A. Garfield

Real leaders are ordinary people with extraordinary determinations.

—John Seaman Garns

A good leader takes a little more than his share of blame; a little less than his share of credit.

—Arnold Glasow

It doesn't take great men to do things, but it is doing things that makes men great.

—Arnold Glasow

The RIGHT Thing to Say

In all legislative assemblies, the greater the number compos-
ing them may be, the fewer will be the men who will in
fact direct their proceedings.

—Alexander Hamilton

There is a price tag on human liberty. That price is the
willingness to assume the responsibilities of being free men.
Payment of this price is a personal matter with each of us.
It is not something we can get others to pay for us. To let
others carry the responsibilities of freedom and the work
and worry that accompany them—while we share only in
the benefits—may be a very human impulse, but it is likely
to be fatal.

—Eugene Holman

The greatest thing about man is his ability to transcend
himself, his ancestry, and his environment and to become
what he dreams of being.

—Tully C. Knoles

When the best leader's work is done, the people say, "We
did it ourselves."

—Lao-Tzu

I do the best I know how, the very best I can,
And I mean to keep doing so until the end.
If the end brings me out all right,
What is said against me won't count;

If it brings me out wrong,
All the angels swearing that I was right
Would have made no difference.

—Abraham Lincoln

The officer talking to his men doesn't tell them the enemy's
guns aren't loaded, and that all is pretty near well. The
captain of the ship in a great sea does not send messages
denying that the gale is blowing. The true morale of men
in a crisis is their determination to seize the thing that
menaces them, and look at it, and be done with it.

—Walter Lippmann

The final test of a leader is that he leaves behind him in
other men the conviction and the will to carry on.

—Walter Lippmann

The first method for estimating the intelligence of a ruler is
to look at the men he has around him.

—Niccoló Machiavelli

The world is not perishing for the want of clever or talented
or well-meaning men. It is perishing for the want of men
of courage and resolution who, in devotion to the cause of
right and truth, can rise above personal feeling and private
ambition.

—Robert J. McCracken

Leadership is action, not position.

—Donald McGannon

One person with a belief is a social power equal to ninety-nine who have only interests.

—John Stuart Mill

Never tell people how to do things. Tell them what you want them to achieve, and they will surprise you with their ingenuity.

—George S. Patton

If we are not to shoulder the burdens of leadership in the free world, then who will?

—Ronald Reagan

If you don't stand for something, you will stand for anything.

—Ginger Rogers

The leader for the time being, whoever he may be, is but an instrument, to be used until broken and then to be cast aside; and if he is worth his salt, he will care no more when he is broken than a soldier cares when he is sent where his life is forfeit in order that victory may be won. In the long fight for righteousness, the watchword for all of us is spend and be spent. It is a little matter whether any one man fails or succeeds; but the cause shall not fail, for it is the cause of mankind.

—Theodore Roosevelt

Disaster is ahead of us if we trust to the leadership of men whose souls are seared and whose eyes are blinded, men of cold heart and narrow mind, who believe we can find safety in dull timidity and dull inaction.

—Theodore Roosevelt

Far better it is to dare mighty things, to win glorious triumphs, even though checkered by failure, than to take rank with those poor spirits who neither enjoy much nor suffer much, because they live in the gray twilight that knows not victory or defeat.

—Theodore Roosevelt

A chief is a man who assumes responsibility. He says, "I was beaten," he does not say, "My men were beaten."

—Antoine de Saint-Exupe'ry

Great men rejoice in adversity, just as brave soldiers triumph in war.

—Lucius Annaeus Seneca

The RIGHT Thing to Say

The meaning of history is never apparent to those who make it; a leader in any age or generation is no more than a man who sees somewhat beyond the end of his nose.

—Thomas Sugrue

Only the bold get to the top.

—Publilius Syrus

Reason and judgment are the qualities of a leader.

—Tacitus

To those waiting with bated breath for that favourite media catch-phrase, the U-turn, I have only one thing to say: you turn if you want to. The lady's not turning.

—Margaret Thatcher

If you can't convince them, confuse them.

—Harry S. Truman

Men make history not the other way 'round. In periods where there is no leadership, society stands still. Progress occurs when courageous, skillful leaders seize the opportunity to change things for the better.

—Harry S. Truman

Great men undertake great things because they are great;
and fools because they think them easy.

—Marquis de Vauvenargues

They can conquer who believe they can.

—Virgil

There are two ways of spreading light: to be the candle or
the mirror that reflects it.

—Edith Wharton

It takes vision and courage to create—it takes faith and
courage to prove.

—Owen D. Young

LIBERALS AND LIBERALISM

I said to my Liberal friend that we are fundamentally the same. I spend money like it's my money and you spend money like it's my money.

—Dick Armey

Envy so often motivates the Left in its quest for redistribution. The economy is not a zero-sum game, and the wealth of a Bill Gates or a Michael Jordan does not take anything away from me. Indeed the wealth of others enhances my life.

—Robert Bork

The liberals can understand everything but people who don't understand them.

—Lenny Bruce

The salient economic assumptions of liberalism are socialist.

—William F. Buckley, Jr.

The judgments that liberals render on public issues, domestic and foreign, are as predictable as the salivation of Pavlovian dogs.

—James Burnham

Of course, almost every Democrat thinks the sovereign remedy for any of our ills is the appropriation of public money.

—Calvin Coolidge

A liberal is a man who is willing to spend somebody else's money.

—Carter Glass

Your liberal is an eternal sixteen-year-old, forever rebellious, forever oblivious to the nasty realities of life, forever looking forward to some impossible revolution in human nature.

—Tony Hendra

Nothing appeals to intellectuals more than the feeling that they represent 'the people.' Nothing, as a rule, is further from the truth.

—Paul Johnson

The person who is in the weakest moral position to attack the state is he who has largely ignored its potential for evil while strongly backing its expansion on humanitarian grounds and is only stirred to protest when he falls foul of it through his own negligence.

—Paul Johnson

A rich man told me recently that a liberal is a man who tells other people what to do with their money.

—LeRoi Jones

A liberal is one who says it's all right for an 18-year-old girl to perform in a pornographic movie as long as she gets paid minimum wage.

—Irving Kristol

A Progressive is one who is in favor of more taxes instead of less, more bureaus and jobholders, more paternalism and meddling, more regulation of private affairs and less liberty. In general, he would be inclined to regard the repeal of any tax as outrageous.

—Henry Mencken

At the core of liberalism is the spoiled child—miserable, as all spoiled children are, unsatisfied, demanding, ill-disciplined, despotic, and useless. Liberalism is a philosophy of sniveling brats.

—P. J. O'Rourke

All organizations that are not actually right-wing will over time become left-wing.

—John O'Sullivan

The real destroyer of the liberties of the people is he who spreads among them bounties, donations and benefits.

—Plutarch

It isn't that Liberals are ignorant. It's just that they know so much that isn't so.

—Ronald Reagan

Let us have the courage to speak the truth: Policies that increase dependency and break up families are not progressive; they're reactionary, even though they are invariably promoted, passed, and carried out in the name of fairness, generosity, and compassion.

—Ronald Reagan

Some of you may remember that in my early days I was a sort of a bleeding heart liberal. Then I became a man and put away childish ways.

—Ronald Reagan

Today there is an increasing number who can't see a fat man standing beside a thin one without automatically coming to the conclusion the fat man got that way by taking advantage of the thin one.

—Ronald Reagan

The RIGHT Thing to Say

I can remember way back, when a Liberal was generous
with his own money.

—Will Rogers

Liberalism has been supposed to advocate liberty; but what
the advanced parties that still call themselves liberal now
advocate is control, control over property, trade, wages,
hours of work, meat and drink, amusements...and it is only
on the subject of marriage...that liberalism is growing more
and more liberal.

—George Santayana

A man's liberties are none the less aggressed upon because
those who coerce him do so in the belief that he will be
benefited.

—Herbert Spencer

LIFE

What is the use of living, if it be not to strive for noble causes and to make this muddled world a better place to live in after we are gone?

—Winston Churchill

The lowest ebb is the turn of the tide.

—Henry Wadsworth Longfellow

MEDIA

Saying the *Washington Post* is just a newspaper is like saying Rasputin was just a country priest.

—Patrick Buchanan

A bullpen seething with mischief. (On reporters)

—George Bush

Journalism consists in buying white paper at two cents a pound and selling it at ten cents a pound.

—Charles A. Dana

Why is the press America's showcase for freedom? Because just about everything else has been regulated.

—Cullen Hightower

People everywhere confuse
What they read in newspapers with news.

—A. J. Liebling

The bigger the information media, the less courage and freedom they allow. Bigness means weakness.

—Eric Sevareid

This generation, raised on "Eyewitness News," conditioned by the instant replay, and spared the illumination that comes from tedious historical study, tends to be even more ahistorical than most.

—Harry S. Truman

POLITICS, POLITICIANS, AND ELECTIONS

There is no worse heresy than that the office sanctifies the holder of it.

—Lord Acton

A candidate running for Congress hired two assistants: one to dig up the facts and the other to bury them.

—Anonymous

Vote for the man who promises least; he'll be the least disappointing.

—Bernard Baruch

Politics, n. A strife of interests masquerading as a contest of principles.

—Ambrose Bierce

Politics is not an exact science.

—Otto von Bismarck

In politics, an absurdity is not an impediment.

—Napoleon Bonaparte

Your representative owes you, not his industry only, but his judgment; and he betrays, instead of serving you, if he sacrifices it to your opinion.

—Edmund Burke

It is not a smear, if you please, if you point out the record of your opponent.

—Murray Chotiner

Politics are almost as exciting as war and quite as dangerous. In war you can only be killed once, but in politics many times.

—Winston Churchill

Nothing is more dangerous…than to live in the temperamental atmosphere of a Gallup Poll, always feeling one's pulse and taking one's temperature.

—Winston Churchill

It is no good going to the country solely on the platform of your opponents' mistakes.

—Winston Churchill

He is asked to stand, he wants to sit, he is expected to lie.

—Winston Churchill

Political ability is the ability to foretell what is going to happen tomorrow, next week, next month and next year. And to have the ability afterwards to explain why it didn't happen.

—Winston Churchill

A politician thinks of the next election; a statesman thinks of the next generation.

—James Freeman Clarke

What is the use of being elected or re-elected unless you stand for something?

—Grover Cleveland

In politics, what begins in fear usually ends in folly.

—Samuel Taylor Coleridge

Politics ought to be the part-time profession of every citizen who would protect the rights and privileges of free people and who would preserve what is good and fruitful in our national heritage.

—Dwight D. Eisenhower

A politician is a person with whose politics you don't agree.
If you agree with him he is a statesman.

—David Lloyd George

Politics is the science of how who gets what, when and why.

—Sidney Hillman

Men play at being God, but lacking God's experience they
wind up as politicians.

—Harry William King

Public interest is a term used by every politician to support
his ideas.

—W. M. Kiplinger

The first method for estimating the intelligence of a ruler is
to look at the men he has around him.

—Niccoló Machiavelli

America is the only country in the world where you can go
on the air and kid politicians—and where politicians go on
the air and kid the people.

—Groucho Marx

The RIGHT Thing to Say

Nothing is politically right which is morally wrong.

—Daniel O'Connell

Do you ever get the feeling that the only reason we have elections is to find out if the polls were right?

—Robert Orben

In our time there is no such thing as 'keeping out of politics.' All issues are political issues and politics itself is a mass of schizophrenia.

—George Orwell

Public office is the last refuge of the scoundrel.

—Boies Penrose

I used to say that politics was the second oldest profession, and I have come to know that it bears a gross similarity to the first.

—Ronald Reagan

The trouble with practical jokes is that very often they get elected.

—Will Rogers

A politician should have three hats. One for throwing in the ring, one for talking through, and one for pulling rabbits out of if elected.

—Carl Sandburg

A politician is one that would circumvent God.

—William Shakespeare

Bad politicians are sent to Washington by good people who don't vote.

—William Simon

An independent is the guy who wants to take politics out of politics.

—Adlai Stevenson

Censure is the tax a man pays to the public for being eminent.

—Jonathan Swift

I always cheer up immediately if an attack is particularly wounding because I think, well, if they attack one personally, it means they have not a single political argument left.

—Margaret Thatcher

It is not the business of politicians to please everyone.

—Margaret Thatcher

In politics if you want anything said, ask a man. If you want anything done, ask a woman.

—Margaret Thatcher

A good politician with nerve and a program that is right can win in the face of the stiffest opposition.

—Harry S. Truman

Voters don't decide issues, they decide who will decide issues.

—George F. Will

If you think too much about being re-elected, it is very difficult to be worth re-electing.

—Woodrow Wilson

POWER

Power tends to corrupt and absolute power corrupts absolutely.

—Lord Acton

No one with absolute power can be trusted to give it up even in part.

—Louis D. Brandeis

Power gradually extirpates from the mind every humane and gentle nature.

—Edmund Burke

Those who have once been intoxicated with power, and have derived any kind of emolument from it, even but from one year can never willingly abandon it.

—Edmund Burke

As wealth is power, so all power will infallibly draw wealth to itself by some means or other.

—Edmund Burke

Society cannot exist unless a controlling power upon will and appetite be placed somewhere, and the less of it there is within the more there must be without.

—Edmund Burke

The greater the power, the more dangerous the abuse.

—Edmund Burke

Power intoxicates men. When a man is intoxicated by alcohol he can recover, but when intoxicated by power he seldom recovers.

—James F. Byrnes

Those in power want only to perpetuate it.

—William O. Douglas

A single seemingly powerless person who dares to cry out the word of truth and to stand behind it with all his person and all his life has, surprisingly, greater power, though formally disenfranchised, than do thousands of anonymous voters.

—Vaclav Havel

The love of liberty is the love of others, the love of power is the love of ourselves.

—William Hazlitt

The descent to hell is easy, and those who begin by worshipping power soon worship evil.

—C. S. Lewis

The question which, in all ages, has disturbed mankind and brought on them the greatest part of those mischiefs which have ruined cities, depopulated countries, and disordered the peace of the world, has been, not whether there be power in the world, not whence it came, but who should have it.

—John Locke

The essence of Government is power; and power, lodged as it must be in human hands, will ever be liable to abuse.

—James Madison

The truth is that all men having power ought to be mistrusted.

—James Madison

In framing a government which is to be administered by men over men, the great difficulty lies in this: you must first enable the government to control the governed; and in the next place, oblige it to control itself.

—James Madison

Politics are always a struggle for power, disguised and modified by prudence, reason and moral pretext.

—William H. Mallock

Political power grows out of the barrel of a gun.

—Mao Zedong

The urge to save humanity is almost always only a false-face for the urge to rule it.

—H. L. Mencken

The only purpose for which power can be rightfully exercised over any member of a civilized community, against his will, is to prevent harm to others. His own good, either physical or moral, is not a sufficient warrant.

—John Stuart Mill

He is the best of men who dislikes power.

—Mohammed

Unlimited power is apt to corrupt the minds of those who possess it.

—William Pitt the Younger

The most dangerous form of inebriation results from too much power.

—Frank Tyger

PROGRESS

Man masters nature not by force but by understanding.

—J. Bronowski

Progress consists largely of learning to apply laws and truths that have always existed.

—John Allan May

Advance from the inferior to the superior must seem as real and certain as anything in the laws of nature.

—Robert Nisbet

PUBLIC OPINION

Public opinion is the last refuge of a politician without any opinion.

—Mark Bonham Carter

A straw vote only shows which way the hot air blows.

—O. P. Henry

RACE

Race should not be a source of power or advantage or disadvantage for anyone in a free society. This was one of the most important lessons of the original civil rights movement.

—Shelby Steele

REVOLUTION

The Revolution is like Saturn—it eats its own children.

—Georg Büchner

Nothing is clearer in history than the adoption by successful rebels of the methods they were accustomed to condemn in the forces they deposed.

—Will Durant

Revolutions are apt to take their color from the regime they overthrow.

—Richard H. Tawney

RIGHTS AND RESPONSIBILITIES

There has been in recent years excessive emphasis on a citizen's rights and inadequate stress upon his duties and responsibilities.

—Paxton Blair

Nations begin to dig their own graves when men talk more of human rights and less of human duties.

—William J. H. Boetcker

They (the makers of the Constitution) conferred, as against the Government, the right to be let alone—the most comprehensive of rights and the right most valued by civilized men.

—Louis D. Brandeis

The only thing necessary for the triumph of evil is for good men to do nothing.

—Edmund Burke

Perhaps it is better to be irresponsible and right than to be responsible and wrong.

—Winston Churchill

Rights! There are no rights whatever without corresponding duties.

—Samuel Taylor Coleridge

Never mind your happiness; do your duty.

—Will Durant

This country was not built by men who relied on somebody else to take care of them. It was built by men who relied on themselves, who dared to shape their own lives, who had enough courage to blaze new trails—enough confidence in themselves to take the necessary risks.

—J. Ollie Edmunds

No man has a natural right to commit aggression on the natural rights of another; and this is all from which the laws ought to restrain him.

—Thomas Jefferson

Nothing then is unchangeable but the inherent and inalienable rights of man.

—Thomas Jefferson

The RIGHT Thing to Say

If a man hasn't discovered something that he will die for, he isn't fit to live.

—Martin Luther King, Jr.

The personal right to acquire property, which is a natural right, gives to property, when acquired, a right to protection, as a social right.

—James Madison

Everyone who receives the protection of society owes a return for the benefit.

—John Stuart Mill

The first requisite of a good citizen in this republic of ours is that he shall be able and willing to pull his weight.

—Theodore Roosevelt

It is easy to dodge our responsibilities, but we cannot dodge the consequences of dodging our responsibilities.

—Sir Josiah Stamp

The dichotomy between personal liberties and property rights is a false one. Property does not have rights. People have rights.

—Potter Stewart

In fact, a fundamental interdependence exists between the personal right to liberty and the personal right in property.

—Potter Stewart

RONALD REAGAN

America's growing self-respect went a long way to erase the masochism generated by the Vietnam debacle, and enabled Reagan, who had no inhibitions about the legitimate use of America's enormous power, to perform on the world stage with growing aplomb. He was not a rash man, and certainly not a bellicose man, but he was a staunch believer in absolute values of conduct with a clear view of the difference between right and wrong in international affairs. When he felt the need to act, he acted; not without careful deliberation, but without any feeling of guilt or *arrierespensees*.

—Paul Johnson

If you ask about a characteristic of Ronald Reagan it is that he had these certain things he believed in and he just didn't change. That was his great strength.

—George P. Schultz

SCIENCE

It was naïve of the 19th century optimists to expect paradise from technology—and it is equally naïve of the 20th century pessimists to make technology the scapegoat for such old shortcomings as man's blindness, cruelty, immaturity, greed and sinful pride.

—Peter F. Drucker

Modern man worships at the temple of science, but science tells him only what is possible, not what is right.

—Milton S. Eisenhower

Science cannot bear the thought that there is an important natural phenomenon which it cannot hope to explain even with unlimited time and money.

—Robert Johnson

SOCIALISM AND COMMUNISM

What was wrong with communism wasn't aberrant leadership, it was communism.

—William F. Buckley, Jr.

Socialize the individual's surplus and you socialize his spirit and creativeness; you cannot paint the Mona Lisa by assigning one dab each to a thousand painters.

—William F. Buckley, Jr.

Government of the duds, by the duds, and for the duds. (On Socialism)

—Winston Churchill

The difference between our outlook and the Socialist outlook is the difference between the ladder and the queue. We are for the ladder. Let all try their best to climb. They are for the queue.

—Winston Churchill

A ghoul descending from a pile of skulls. (On Communism)

—Winston Churchill

Socialism is the philosophy of failure, the creed of ignorance and the gospel of envy.

—Winston Churchill

...[S]ocial engineering has been the salient delusion and the greatest curse of the modern age. In the twentieth century it has killed scores of millions of innocent people, in Soviet Russia, Nazi Germany, Communist China and elsewhere. But it is the last thing which Western democracies, with all their faults, have ever espoused. On the contrary. Social engineering is the creation of millenarian intellectuals who believe they can refashion the universe by the light of their unaided reason.

—Paul Johnson

...[T]he century's most radical vice...the notion that human beings can be shoveled around like concrete.

—Paul Johnson

The typical socialist...a prim little man with a white-collar job, usually a secret teetotaler and often with vegetarian leanings.

—George Orwell

Marxism is too uncertain of its grounds to be a science. I do not know a movement more self-centered and further removed from the facts than Marxism.

—Boris Pasternak

The term 'democratic socialist' makes as much sense as 'pregnant virginity.'

—Russell Prowse

How do you tell a Communist? Well it's someone who reads Marx and Lenin. And how do you tell an anti-Communist? It's someone who understands Marx and Lenin.

—Ronald Reagan

All Socialism involves slavery.

—Herbert Spencer

The dictatorship of the Communist Party is maintained by recourse to every form of violence.

—Leon Trotsky

The saddest illusion of revolutionary socialists is that revolution itself will transform the nature of human beings.

—Shirley Williams

SURVIVAL

We must resolutely train ourselves to feel that the survival of Man on the Earth, much more of our own nation or culture or class is not worth having unless it can be had by honourable and merciful means.... Nothing is more likely to destroy a species or a nation than a determination to survive at all costs.

—C. S. Lewis

TAXES AND SPENDING

A power in the individuals who compose legislatures, to fish up wealth from the people, by nets of their own weaving...will corrupt legislative, executive, and judicial public servants.

—John Adams

There is just one thing I can promise you about the outer-space program: your dollars will go farther.

—Wernher von Braun

To tax and to please, no more than to love and to be wise, is not given to man.

—Edmund Burke

The Congress will push me to raise taxes and I'll say no, and they'll push and I'll say no, and they'll push again, and I'll say to them, "Read my lips: no new taxes."

—George Bush

There is one difference between a tax collector and a taxidermist—the taxidermist leaves the hide.

—Mortimer Caplan

The idea that a nation can tax itself into prosperity is one of the cruelest delusions which has ever befuddled the human mind.

—Winston Churchill

The point to remember is what the government gives it must first take away.

—John S. Coleman

Nothing is easier than spending the public money. It does not appear to belong to anybody.

—Calvin Coolidge

Collecting more taxes than is absolutely necessary is legalized robbery.

—Calvin Coolidge

The hardest thing in the world to understand is the income tax.

—Albert Einstein

As quickly as you start spending federal money in large amounts, it looks like free money.

—Dwight D. Eisenhower

Men's common guise is always to lay the burden on some other back.

—English proverb, c. 1515

Some taxpayers close their eyes, some stop their ears, some shut their mouths, but all pay through the nose.

—Evan Esar

But in this world, nothing is certain but death and taxes.

—Benjamin Franklin

The political function of the income taxes, which is served by their being complex, is to provide a means whereby the members of Congress who have anything whatsoever to do with taxation can raise campaign funds.

—Milton Friedman

I'm proud to be paying taxes to the U.S. The only thing is—I could be just as proud for half the money.

—Arthur Godfrey

Balancing the budget is like going to heaven. Everybody wants to do it, but nobody wants to do what you have to do to get there.

—Phil Gramm

It is no part of the State's duty to facilitate the spiritual redemption of rich men by impoverishing them in this life.

—John Grigg

Do we imagine that our assessments operate equally? Nothing can be more contrary to the fact. Wherever a discretionary power is lodged in any set of men over the property of their neighbors, they will abuse it.

—Alexander Hamilton

Taxes are not levied for the benefit of the taxed.

—Robert A. Heinlein

Blessed are the young, for they shall inherit the national debt.

—Herbert Hoover

We will spend and spend, and tax and tax, and elect and elect.

—Harry L. Hopkins

Public money is like holy water; everyone helps himself.

—Italian saying

It is incumbent on every generation to pay its own debts as it goes.

—Thomas Jefferson

The greatest security against the introduction of corrupt practices and principles into our government is make [them keep]...public expenses down to their minimum.

—Thomas Jefferson

Tax reform means, "Don't tax you, don't tax me. Tax that fellow behind the tree."

—Russell Long

The power to tax involves the power to destroy.

—John Marshall

There are no uncontrollable outlays except for debt interest. Outlays are what they are due to legislation.

—Paul W. McCracken

Prosperity of the middling and lower orders depends upon the fortunes and light taxes of the rich.

—Andrew Mellon

When a new source of taxation is found it never means, in practice, that an old source is abandoned. It merely means that the politicians have two ways of milking the taxpayer where they had only one before.

—Henry Mencken

If Patrick Henry thought that taxation without representation was bad he should see how bad it is with representation.

—Old Farmer's Almanac

The budget grows because, like zygotes and suburban lawns, it was designed to do nothing else.

—P. J. O'Rourke

Taxation without representation is tyranny.

—James Otis

We do not face large deficits because American families are undertaxed; we face those deficits because the federal government overspends.

—Ronald Reagan

The taxpayer—that's someone who works for the federal government but doesn't have to take a civil-service exam.

—Ronald Reagan

The size of the Federal budget is not an appropriate barometer of social conscience or charitable concern.

—Ronald Reagan

Taxation under every form presents but a choice of evils.

—David Ricardo

The income tax has made more liars out of the American people than golf has.

—Will Rogers

Foreign Aid—taxing poor people in rich countries for the benefit of rich people in poor countries.

—Bernard Rosenberg

An unlimited power to tax involves, necessarily, the power to destroy.

—Daniel Webster

It is always other the "other fellow's" programs that should be cut. Unfortunately, there are not enough "other fellows" to go around.

—Murray Weidenbaum

TRUTH

As scarce as truth is, the supply has always been in excess of the demand.

—Josh Billings

The truth is uncontrovertible. Panic may resent it; ignorance may deride it; malice may destroy it, but there it is.

—Winston Churchill

The object of the superior man is truth. Food is not his object. The superior man is anxious lest he should not get truth; he is not anxious lest poverty should come upon him.

—Confucius

Those who know the truth are not equal to those who love it.

—Confucius

Truth is generally the best vindication against slander.

—Abraham Lincoln

Of course it's the same old story. Truth usually is the same old story.

—Margaret Thatcher

TYRANNY

Destiny, n. A tyrant's excuse for crime and a fool's excuse for failure.

—Ambrose Bierce

Tyrants seldom want pretexts.

—Edmund Burke

Bad laws are the worst sort of tyranny.

—Edmund Burke

The evils of tyranny are rarely seen, but by him who resists it.

—John Hay

What has always made the state a hell on earth has been precisely that man has tried to make it his heaven.

—Friedrich Holderlin

Despotism violates the moral frontier, an invasion violates the geographic frontier.

—Victor Hugo

Rebellion to tyrants is obedience to God.

—Thomas Jefferson

Force is the vital principle and immediate parent of depotism.

—Thomas Jefferson

If ever this vast country is brought under a single government, it will be one of the most extensive corruption.

—Thomas Jefferson

A police state finds it cannot command grain to grow.

—John F. Kennedy

"Useful," and "necessity" was always "the tyrant's plea."

—C. S. Lewis

Dictators are rulers who always look good until the last ten minutes.

—Jan Masaryk

The worst tyranny is that of misapplied laws.

—Metternich

Tyranny, like hell, is not easily conquered.

—Thomas Paine

Tyranny is always better organized than freedom.

—Charles Peguy

If we will not be governed by God, we must be governed by tyrants.

—William Penn

Necessity is the plea for every infringement of human freedom. It is the argument of tyrants, it is the creed of slaves.

—William Pitt the Younger

When you stop a dictator there are always risks. But there are greater risks in not stopping a dictator.

—Margaret Thatcher

VIRTUE

The superior man thinks always of virtue; the common man thinks of comfort.

—Confucius

We acquire virtue in much the same way we acquire other skills, by practicing the craft.

—Clarence Thomas

WAR AND PEACE

For a war to be just, three conditions are necessary—public authority, just cause, right motive.

—Thomas Aquinas

In the choice of a general, we should regard his skill rather than his virtue—for few have military skill, but many have virtue.

—Aristotle

Peace, n. In international affairs, a period of cheating between two periods of fighting.

—Ambrose Bierce

War is the second worst activity of mankind, the worst being acquiescence in slavery.

—William F. Buckley, Jr.

Wars are just to those for whom they are necessary.

—Edmund Burke

Armaments do not, generally speaking, cause wars. This notion, the logical crux of all arguments in favor of disarmament, turns the casual relationship upside down. Actually it is wars or conflicts threatening war, that cause armaments, not the reverse.

—James Burnham

I believe it is peace for our time...peace with honor.

—Neville Chamberlain

If you will not fight for the right when you can easily win without bloodshed, if you will not fight when your victory will be sure, you may come to the moment when you will have to fight with all the odds against you and only a precarious chance for survival.

—Winston Churchill

Never give in. Never, never, never, never! Never yield in any way, great or small, except to convictions of honor and good sense. Never yield to force and the apparently over-whelming might of the enemy.

—Winston Churchill

There are many things worse than war. Slavery is worse than war. Dishonor is worse than war.

—Winston Churchill

Victory at all costs, victory in spite of all terror, victory however long and hard the road may be, for without victory there is no survival.

—Winston Churchill

Appeasement in itself may be good or bad according to circumstances. Appeasement from strength is magnani-mous and noble and might be the surest and perhaps the only road to world peace.

—Winston Churchill

We must be prepared.... [I]t is good to be patient, it is good to be circumspect, it is good to be peace-loving—but it is not enough. We must be strong, we must be self-reliant.

—Winston Churchill

The name of peace is sweet and the thing itself good, but between peace and slavery there is the greatest difference.

—Marcus Cicero

We face a hostile ideology—global in scope, atheistic in character, ruthless in purpose, and insidious in method.

—Dwight D. Eisenhower

In the final choice a soldier's pack is not so heavy a burden as a prisoner's chains.

—Dwight D. Eisenhower

History does not long entrust the care of freedom to the weak or the timid. We must acquire proficiency in defense and display stamina in purpose.

—Dwight D. Eisenhower

Even peace may be purchased at too high a price.

—Benjamin Franklin

Thank heaven for the military-industrial complex. Its ultimate aim is peace for our time.

—Barry Goldwater

The art of war is simple enough. Find out where your enemy is. Get at him as soon as you can. Strike at him as hard as you can, and keep moving on.

—Ulysses S. Grant

War is a dreadful thing, but there are things more dreadful even than war; one of them is dishonor.

—William Randolph Hearst

Once we have a war there is only one thing to do. It must be won. For defeat brings worse things than any that can ever happen in war.

—Ernest Hemingway

We shall more certainly preserve peace when it is well understood that we are prepared for war.

—Andrew Jackson

Whatever enables us to go to war, secures our peace.

—Thomas Jefferson

Peace with all nations, and the right which that gives us with respect to all nations, are our object.

—Thomas Jefferson

...[N]ot peace at any price. There is a peace more destructive to the manhood of living man than war is destructive of his material body. Chains are worse than bayonets.

—Douglas W. Jerrold

If there is any one lesson to be plainly derived from the experiences we have had with disarmament in the past half-century, it is that armaments are a function and not a cause of political tensions and that no limitation of armaments on a multilateral scale can be effected as long as the political problems are not tackled and regulated in some realistic way.

—George Kennan

The mere absence of war is not peace.

—John F. Kennedy

It is an unfortunate fact that we can only secure peace by preparing for war.

—John F. Kennedy

Only when arms are sufficient beyond doubt can we be certain without doubt that they will never be employed.

—John F. Kennedy

Outlawing all atomic weapons would be a magnificent gesture. However, it should be remembered that Gettysburg had a local ordinance forbidding the discharge of firearms.

—Homer D. King

You can't win through negotiations what you can't win on the battlefield.

—Henry Kissinger

St. Paul...approved of capital punishment—he says "the magistrate bears the sword and should bear the sword." It is recorded that the soldiers who came to St. John the Baptist asking, "What shall we do?" were told not to leave the army. When Our Lord Himself praised the Centurion He never hinted that the military profession was in itself sinful. This has been the general view of Christendom. Pacifism is a recent and local variation. We must of course respect and tolerate Pacifists, but I think their view erroneous.

—C. S. Lewis

It is fatal to enter any war without the will to win it.

—General Douglas MacArthur

It is not armaments that cause war, but war that causes armaments.

—Salvador de Madariaga

A certain degree of preparation for war...affords also the best security for the continuance of peace.

—James Madison

If man does find the solution for world peace it will be the most revolutionary reversal of his record we have ever known.

—George C. Marshall

There is no record in history of a nation that ever gained anything valuable by being unable to defend itself.

—H. L. Mencken

That expression "positive neutrality" is a contradiction in terms. There can be no more positive neutrality than there can be a vegetarian tiger.

—V. K. Krishna Menon

War is an ugly thing, but not the ugliest of things: the decayed and degraded state of moral and patriotic feeling which thinks nothing worth a war, is worse.

—John Stuart Mill

A good general not only sees the way to victory; he also knows when victory is impossible.

—Polybius

Of the four wars in my lifetime, none came about because the U.S. was too strong.

—Ronald Reagan

History teaches that wars begin when governments believe the price of aggression is cheap.

—Ronald Reagan

To blame the military for war makes about as much sense as suggesting that we get rid of cancer by getting rid of doctors.

—Ronald Reagan

Nations do not mistrust each other because they are armed; they are armed because they mistrust each other.

—Ronald Reagan

The more you sweat in peace, the less you bleed in war.

—Hyman Rickover

If I must choose between peace and righteousness, I choose righteousness.

—Theodore Roosevelt

Generally peace tells for righteousness; but if there is conflict between the two, then our fealty is due first to the cause of righteousness.

—Theodore Roosevelt

If peace cannot be maintained with honor, it is no longer peace.

—Lord John Russell

What deters war is the completeness and integrity of the U.S. deterrent.

—James R. Schlesinger

Worse than war is the fear of war.

—Lucius Annaeus Seneca

The best way not to use nuclear weapons is to be prepared to use them.

—Samuel S. Stratton

The RIGHT Thing to Say

We should provide in peace what we need in war.

—Publilius Syrus

War is a bad thing: but to submit to the dictation of other states is worse.... Freedom, if we hold fast to it, will ultimately restore our losses, but submission will mean permanent loss of all that we value. To you who call yourselves men of peace, I say: You are not safe unless you have men of action at your side.

—Thucydides

War is not so onerous as slavery.

—Marquis de Vauvenargues

Let him who desires peace prepare for war.

—Vegetius

To be prepared for War is one of the most effectual means of preserving peace.

—George Washington

There is nothing so likely to produce peace as to be well prepared to meet an enemy.

—George Washington

The absolute pacifist is a bad citizen; times come when force must be used to uphold right, justice and ideals.

—Alfred North Whitehead

INDEX OF NAMES

IF YOU ENJOYED THIS BOOK

you may want to join the organization that made it possible. Citizens United is a non-profit, non-partisan educational organization based in Fairfax, Virginia, with 100,000 members nationwide.

Kirby Wilbur, lead author of Say the RIGHT Thing, is director and officer of Citizens United, which was founded by co-author Floyd Brown in 1988, and dedicated to restoring government to citizen control. Floyd Brown founded Citizens United because of his desire to communicate conservative ideas to America's citizens. Through a combination of education, publishing, and grassroots activism, Citizens United seeks to reassert the values of limited government, freedom of enterprise, strong families, and national sovereignty and security.

For more information on Citizens United, fill out the coupon and mail or fax to 703-591-2505.